PAPER PLATE ANGEL DECORATIONS

Materials Needed:
- Crayons, markers, or colored pencils
- Scissors
- Glue
- Tape
- Yellow pipe cleaner
- Construction paper
- Large thin paper plate with ridges

Instructions:
Color then cut out the patterns on page 17.
Take a paper plate and fold it in half.
Next, fold it in half again to form a triangle.
Tape the paper plate sides together to form a cone,
which can stand upright. Cut out 2 triangle shapes from
another paper plate to create angel arms.
Cut out hands from construction paper and glue to the wide end of the arms.
Fold the point of the triangle to create a tab to use to attach the arms.
Wrap the arms around the paper plate and tape the tab to the back of the angel.
Glue the cut-out wing patterns over the arm tabs on the back. Glue on the head.
Take the pipe cleaner and twist to make a circle for the halo with a stem in the back.
Place the halo stem in between the creases of the paper plate on the top to secure the halo.

COFFEE FILTER ANGELS

Materials Needed:
- 3 Coffee filters
- Ribbon
- Large cotton ball or small styrofoam balls
- Glitter
- Scissors
- Glue

Instructions:
Fold coffee filter in half and then in half again to form a triangle for the body.
Fluff the body so it stands like a cone. Wrap a second coffee filter around a large cotton ball
or a styrofoam ball to form the head and then secure with ribbon.
Insert the triangular body into the center of the head coffee filter and glue in place.
Take remaining coffee filter and cut in half. Fold each half in half again to form the wings.
Glue one half on each side of the body of your angel.
Decorate your angel using glue and glitter.

ADVENT WREATH WITH CANDLES

Materials Needed:
- 5 Toilet paper rolls
- Scissors
- Tape
- Glue
- Construction paper
- Decorative paper
- Paper plate

Instructions:

Using a paper plate, draw a circle on a large square
sheet of construction paper.

Cut out the circle to use as your candle tray.

Cut out the patterns on page 15.

For additional leaves and berries, page 16 patterns can also be used.

Glue the leaves and berries to the circular candle tray leaving room
for 4 of the candles to be spaced symmetrically around the circle and the remaining candle in the middle of the tray.

Cut 4-inch strips of decorative or construction paper to wrap around the toilet paper rolls and then secure with tape.

Glue one candle pattern without the flame for each of the wrapped rolls.

Each week after church, glue the flame to the appropriate candle in the order described on page 3
until the Christ candle is finally "lit."

ADVENT CHRISTMAS TREE CALENDAR

Materials Needed:
- Scissors
- Glue
- 25 Toilet paper rolls
- Pom poms or other decorations
- Construction paper
- 25 Mini candy bars

Instructions For Treats:

Trace the toilet paper roll on construction paper to make circles.

Cut out 25 circles and number them 1 to 25.

Cut out the candy bar wrapper patterns on page 28.

Wrap the patterns around mini candy bars and secure with tape.

Instructions For Tree:

TREE:

Lay out the toilet paper rolls to create a tree shape starting with 1 roll
at the top, then a row of 2, then a row of 3, and so on until your shape
is 6 rolls wide.

Glue the bottom of each row as you go so they stick together.

Cover the outer tree shape with green construction paper.

TRUNK:

Arrange toilet paper rolls 2 rolls wide by 2 rolls high to form the tree trunk.

Glue the 4 rolls together.

Cover the trunk with green construction paper.

Glue tree trunk to base of tree shape.

Glue assembled tree and trunk to a large sheet of construction paper so it has a back.

Fill each toilet paper roll with candy.

Glue numbered circles to cover the front of each toilet paper roll, hiding the candy.

Decorate the sides of the tree with your chosen decorations.

Mount the project on a bulletin board or lay flat.

For each day in December, until Christmas Day, open the corresponding numbered toilet paper roll to retrieve the candy treat.

WHAT IS ADVENT?

The **Advent season** begins on a Sunday, four weeks before Christmas Eve. It is the time that Christians prepare for the birth of Christ. It is a special time for families to celebrate and acknowledge God's incredible gift of sending His Son, Jesus, to earth. Most advent wreaths use three colors of candles including purple, pink, and white. Although, some churches may choose to use royal blue candles instead of purple. Making an advent wreath, lighting candles, and reading scripture are ways we can prepare our hearts leading up to Christmas. The meaning of each candle could be different depending on different church traditions, but the overall preparation of Christ's arrival is what is celebrated among Christians during the special Advent season.

WEEK 1:

The first candle (purple) represents HOPE. Read Romans 15:12-13 ICB.
And Isaiah says, "A new king will come from Jesse's family. He will come to rule over the non-Jews; and the non-Jews will have hope because of him." I pray that the God who gives hope will fill you with much joy and peace while you trust in him. Then your hope will overflow by the power of the Holy Spirit.

WEEK 2:

The second candle (purple) represents PEACE. Read Isaiah 9:6 NIV.
For to us a child is born, to us a son is given, and the government will be on his shoulders. And he will be called Wonderful Counselor, Mighty God, Everlasting Father, Prince of Peace.

WEEK 3:

The third candle (pink) represents JOY. Read Luke 2:8-12 NIV.
And there were shepherds living out in the fields nearby, keeping watch over their flocks at night. An angel of the Lord appeared to them, and the glory of the Lord shone around them, and they were terrified. But the angel said to them, "Do not be afraid. I bring you good news that will cause great joy for all the people. Today in the town of David a Savior has been born to you; he is the Messiah, the Lord. This will be a sign to you: You will find a baby wrapped in cloths and lying in a manger."

WEEK 4:

The fourth candle (purple) represents LOVE. Read John 3:16-17 NIV.
For God so loved the world that he gave his one and only Son, that whoever believes in him shall not perish but have eternal life. For God did not send his Son into the world to condemn the world, but to save the world through him.

CHRISTMAS EVE:

The fifth candle (white) represents CHRIST. Read John 1:29 NIV.
The next day John saw Jesus coming toward him and said, "Look, the Lamb of God, who takes away the sin of the world!"

JINGLE BELLS WREATH ORNAMENT

Materials Needed:

- Crafting wire
- Bells
- Ribbon
- Scissors

Instructions:

Thread crafting wire through bells to form a circle,
leaving excess wire at each end.
Twist excess wire together to secure and trim off remaining wire.
Attach a ribbon to the top and tie to form a hanging loop.
Display on the tree.

BEADED CANDY CANE ORNAMENT

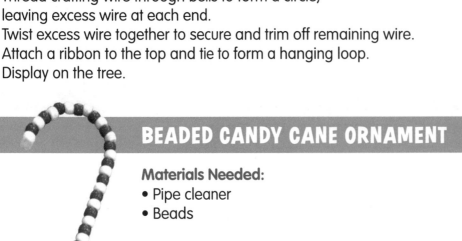

Materials Needed:

- Pipe cleaner
- Beads

Instructions:

Thread beads onto a pipe cleaner.
Form the pipe cleaner into a candy cane shape.
Twist each of the ends so the beads do not fall off.
Proudly display on the tree.

MASON JAR LID ORNAMENT

Materials Needed:

- Photograph
- Scissors
- Glue
- Mason jar lid
- Ribbon

Instructions:

Using the inner lid of the mason jar, trace a circle around a photograph.
Cut out the photograph and glue to the lid.
Glue ribbon around the perimeter of the outer ring of the mason jar lid to decorate.
With ribbon, tie a hanging loop around the outer ring of the mason jar lid.
Add a bow if you'd like.
Insert photo into the mason jar ring and glue to the inner rim.
Proudly display on the tree.

ANGEL NAPKIN RINGS

Materials Needed:
- Scissors
- Glue
- Toilet paper roll
- Napkin

Instructions:
Cut out the pattern on page 20.
Cut a toilet paper roll to form a 2-inch ring.
Glue the pattern around the toilet paper roll.
Roll up a napkin and insert through the ring.
Display on your holiday table.

ANGEL SILVERWARE HOLDERS

Materials Needed:
- Scissors
- Glue
- Toilet paper roll

Instructions:
Cut out the pattern on page 20.
Glue pattern around a toilet paper roll.
Cut along the dotted lines.
Place silverware in the center of the ring.
Display on your holiday table.

5

CUPCAKE LINER TREE GARLAND

Materials Needed:
- Glue
- Ribbon
- Cupcake liners
- Sequins
- Optional: Hole punch

Instructions:

Fold cupcake liners in half and then in half again to form a triangle.

Use three cupcake liner triangles to create a tree shape, inserting the top of the second triangle halfway into the first triangle, and the third triangle halfway into the second triangle and then securing with glue.

Decorate the three layers of your tree with sequins or accent decorations.

Glue the trees to ribbon to form a garland.

Helpful Hint: You can also hole-punch the tops of the trees and thread with ribbon or yarn if desired.

BUTTON WREATH PICTURE ORNAMENT

Materials Needed:
- Scissors
- Glue
- Tape
- Buttons
- Ribbon
- Construction paper
- Photograph

Instructions:

Cut a photograph into a circular shape.

Glue photograph to a piece of construction paper.

Glue buttons around the edges of the photograph.

Cut out a circle around the buttons.

Make a bow out of ribbon and glue to the bottom of the ornament.

Make a hanging loop out of ribbon and tape to the back of the ornament.

SALT DOUGH HANDPRINT ORNAMENT

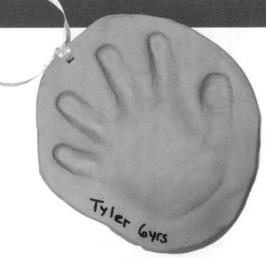

Materials Needed:
- Ribbon
- Permanent marker
- Varnish
- Paint
- Butter knife
- Straw or pencil

Dough Ingredients:
- 2 Cups plain flour
- ½ Cup salt
- ½ Cup water

Instructions:

Mix the dough ingredients in a large bowl.

Roll out to about ¼ inch thickness.

Cut a circular shape out of the dough with butter knife.

Using a straw or pencil, poke a hole in the top of the dough.

Have your child place a hand in the dough pressing down firmly with each finger to create the imprint pattern.

Allow dough to dry approximately 12 hours (thicker ornaments may take longer).

Paint the ornament any color you choose. Once the paint dries, write the child's name and age or current year on the ornament.

Spray with varnish. Thread a ribbon through the hole at the top and tie a knot to form a hanging loop.

HANDPRINT WREATH

Materials Needed:
- Scissors
- Glue
- Construction paper
- Ribbon
- Red and green heavy construction paper or tag board

Instructions:
Have a child trace their right hand on heavy construction paper or tag board.
Cut out the handprint.
Using this as a pattern, trace the handprint on construction paper to make 12 handprints.
Glue the handprints to each other in a circle, overlapping as you go to make a wreath.
Cut out circles to create berries and glue to the wreath.
Attach a ribbon to the top and tie to form a hanging loop.
Have the child write their name and date on the back of the wreath.

Helpful Hints: Wrapping paper and other colors of decorative paper can also be used for creativity. Any decorations can be used to make the wreath more festive.

STAINED GLASS ORNAMENTS

Materials Needed:
- Scissors
- Glue
- X-acto knife
- Decorative paper, cellophane, or tissue paper
- Hole punch
- Ribbon

Instructions:
Using an X-acto knife or razor blade an adult should cut out the center of the patterns on pages 23 and 24.
On the back side of the ornament fill in the trimmed out area with decorative paper, cellophane, or tissue paper and glue in place.
Hole-punch the top of the ornament.
Thread the ornament with ribbon and tie to form a hanging loop.

PAPER PLATE CANDLE WREATH

Materials Needed:
- Scissors
- Glue
- Ribbon
- Paper plate

Instructions:
Cut out the patterns on page 16.
Cut out the center of a paper plate.
Decorate the wreath by wrapping it with ribbon.
Glue on the candle and other patterns
from page 16 (using some or all of them).
Attach a ribbon to the top and tie in a knot to
form a hanging loop.

Helpful Hint: Instead of wrapping ribbon around
the wreath, a child may use crayons or markers to
decorate the white paper plate as they choose.

POPSICLE STICK MANGER SCENE ORNAMENT

Materials Needed:
- Scissors
- Glue
- 4 Popsicle sticks
  (three whole and one cut in half)
- Straw-type basket filler
- Burlap or construction paper
- Ribbon

Instructions:
Cut out the patterns on page 22.
Glue Popsicle sticks to form a manger with two halves as the sides of the manger.
Make a hanging loop with the ribbon and glue to the back of the manger ornament.
Lay the manger on top of burlap or construction paper, then trace and cut out.
Glue the burlap or construction paper cutout to the back of the manger,
making sure to cover the area where the ribbon is attached with glue.
On the front side of the manger, glue the holy family pattern to the bottom Popsicle stick
and the star pattern to the peak of the two top Popsicle sticks.
Glue the straw-type basket filler to the bottom Popsicle stick to create the look of hay.

BABY JESUS IN A MANGER PAPER PLATE CRAFT

Materials Needed:

- Crayons, markers, or colored pencils
- Scissors
- Glue
- Paper plate
- Ribbon

Instructions:

Cut the center out of a paper plate.
Tie a ribbon around the top of the paper plate
to form a hanging loop .
Color and then cut out the patterns on page 22.
Glue the Baby Jesus pattern to the bottom of the
plate and the star to the top (covering the ribbon).

SHEET MUSIC ANGEL ORNAMENTS

Materials Needed:

- Crayons, markers, or colored pencils
- Scissors
- Glue
- Ribbon
- Hole punch

Instructions:

Color and cut out the patterns on page 18.
Cut out the patterns on page 19.
Glue the sheet music wings to the back of the colored angels.
Hole-punch the top.
Attach a ribbon through the hole and tie to form a hanging loop.

DECORATIVE DOOR HANGERS

Materials Needed:
- Crayons, markers, or colored pencils
- Scissors
- Glue
- Construction paper or tag board

Instructions:
Color the patterns on page 27.
Glue the colored patterns to construction paper or tag board.
Cut out the patterns and hang on any door.

SHEET MUSIC ORNAMENTS

Materials Needed:
- Scissors
- Glue
- Ribbon
- Construction paper or tag board
- Hole Punch
- Glitter
- Sequins

Instructions:
Tear out and then glue page 21 to a piece of construction paper or tag board.
Cut out the tree and angel patterns.
Decorate the ornaments.
Punch a hole in the top of each ornament.
Thread the ornament with ribbon and tie in a knot to form a hanging loop.

Helpful Hint: Any decorations will work if you do not have glitter or sequins on hand.

ANGEL CHRISTMAS COASTER SET

Materials Needed:

- Crayons, markers, or colored pencils
- Scissors
- Felt
- Glue
- Laminating paper or laminating machine

Instructions:

Color the coaster patterns on page 14.
Cut out and laminate the colored coasters.
Glue the laminated coasters to felt and let dry.
Cut out the coasters.

Helpful Hint: After you cut out and glue the patterns put them under a heavy book so the coasters dry flat and don't curl.

LUMINARIES

Materials Needed:

- Crayons, markers, or colored pencils
- Scissors
- Tape

Instructions:

Color and then cut out the patterns on page 26.
Tape pattern around an LED tea light.

BOW TIE PASTA GARLAND

Materials Needed:
- Washable finger paint
- Ribbon
- Bow tie pasta

Instructions:
Paint the pasta any color and let dry.
Tie ribbon around the pasta pieces to make garland.

GIFT TAGS

Materials Needed:
- Crayons, markers, or colored pencils
- Scissors
- Ribbon
- Hole punch

Helpful Hint: If you don't have a hole punch, just glue or tape gift tags directly to the packages.

Instructions:
Color and then cut out the patterns on page 31.
Hole-punch the tops of the gift tags.
String with ribbon to create a loop to tie to packages.

TREAT BAG TOPPERS

Materials Needed:
- Crayons, markers, or colored pencils
- Stapler
- Candy
- Cellophane or sandwich bags

Instructions:
Color and cut out the patterns on page 30.
Fold on the dotted lines to form a bag "header" decorated on both sides.
Fill a cellophane or sandwich bag with candy.
Staple the header to the top of the bag to secure and decorate the treat bag.

DECORATIVE GIFT BAGS

Materials Needed:
- Glue
- Scissors
- Brown craft gift bags

Instructions:
Cut out the decoration patterns on page 32.
Arrange and glue to both sides of a craft bag.

Helpful Hints: Bags can be purchased 2 for $1 at most dollar stores.

SCRIPTURE VERSE ORNAMENTS

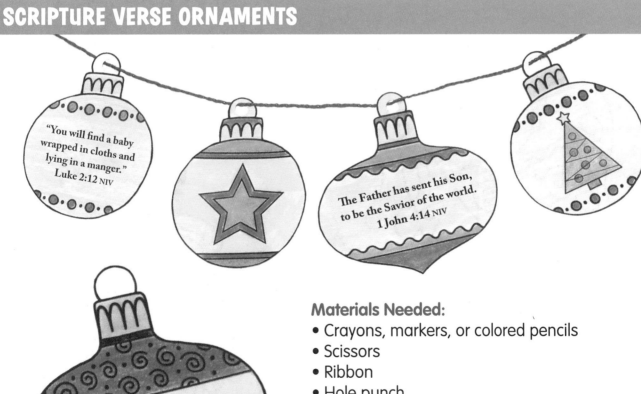

Materials Needed:
- Crayons, markers, or colored pencils
- Scissors
- Ribbon
- Hole punch

Instructions:
Color and then cut out the patterns on page 25.
Hole-punch the tops of the ornaments.
String with ribbon or yarn to make a garland.

To download the songs
and a PDF of this book visit
www.downloadkidsmusic.com
and enter promo code:

ETM1C6

Do not cut patterns. Please photocopy
or use the download code to print
copies from your home computer.

Directions on page 8

Directions on page 1

Directions on page 9

Directions on page 5

NAPKIN RING

SILVERWARE HOLDER

Directions on page 10

Directions on page 8

BABY JESUS IN A MANGER PAPER PLATE CRAFT

Directions on page 9

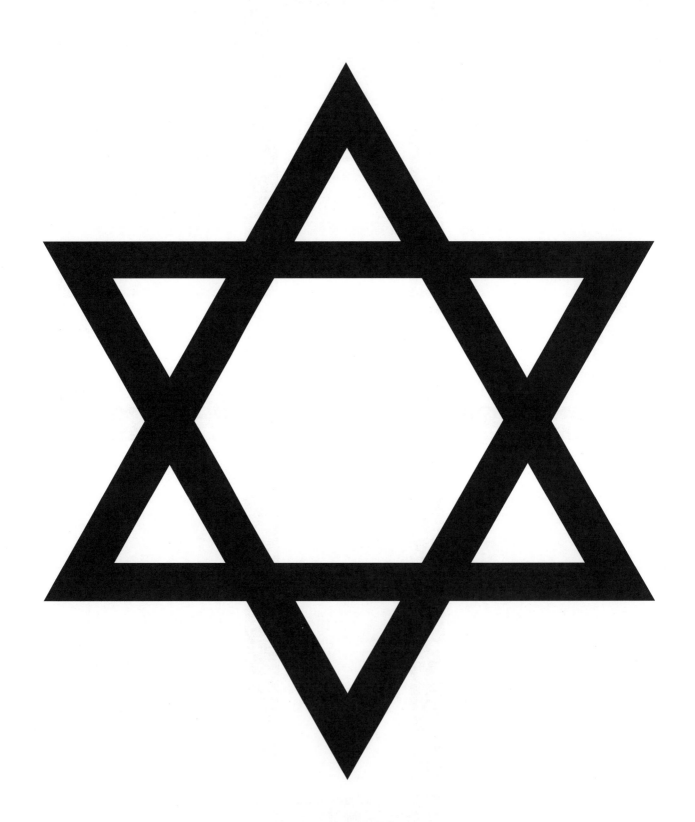

Directions on page 13

The Father has sent his Son, to be the Savior of the world. 1 John 4:14 NIV

"Today in the town of David a Savior has been born to you; he is the Messiah, the Lord." Luke 2:11 NIV

"You will find a baby wrapped in cloths and lying in a manger." Luke 2:12 NIV

Directions on page 10

When the wise men saw the star, they were filled with joy.
Matthew 2:10 ICB

CHRIST THE SAVIOR IS BORN!

Alpha and Omega	SAVIOR	Messiah	SON OF GOD	Wonderful
Everlasting Father	Prince of Peace	COUNSELOR	THE WAY THE TRUTH THE LIFE	Emmanuel
Lamb of God	Rock	Good Shepherd	Light of the World	CHRIST THE LORD

LARGE CANDY BAR WRAPPER GIFT

Materials Needed:
- Crayons, markers or colored pencils
- Scissors
- Tape
- Full-sized candy bar

Instructions:
Color in the candy bar wrapper pattern below.
Cut out the wrapper.
Wrap around a candy bar and secure with tape.

GREAT GIFT IDEA!

Directions on page 12

MERRY CHRISTMAS

JOY *to the* WORLD

O,
Star of *wonder,*
star of *night,*
Star with royal beauty
bright...

O
come
all ye
Faithful
JOYFUL and
triumphant
O COME YE O COME YE TO *Bethlehem*
come and behold Him
born the KING of
Angels O COME LET US ADORE *Him*
Christ the Lord